# Wistful Moments

## Anthology

Bindu Rajiv

BookLeaf Publishing

India | USA | UK

Made with ❤ on the BookLeaf Publishing Platform
www.bookleafpub.in
www.bookleafpub.com

# Dedication

This book is dedicated to my divine guru, parents and family in joining my effort to create a fusion of reality from glimpses of life and abstract thinking.

# Preface

This book is a literary blossoming of my intimate observations of the intricacies of life and the metamorphosis of the current tumultuous world.These poems are contemplary , realistic and gripping into the vagaries of human nature.Each poem is written from my soul and my reflections of life in three decades.Life is a process of evolution.we must learn to celebrate our successes and failures equally in the master fabric of life.

# Acknowledgements

I acknowledge the academic and vernacular support and heartfelt encouragement of my family , friends and my mentor .
I could propose from concept to blueprint effortlessly.

# 1. Youth

I am ready to learn and
work hard to earn
I am in my teens fit for
my blue jeans
look at my gender do i
sound you tender
I am eighteen going to be
nineteen

My desires are coming
out
I am ready to shout my
voice loud
Can you applaud for me
as i reach that stream
to capture the best scene.

# 2. Life

Life is precious.

In one moment death
takes away

Live life in this moment.

Speak words to heal not
hurt.

Help others if you can.

Stay away from
negativity in any form.

Set an example to make

people believe life is to

live.

# 3. True Love

True love purifies the
heart to bring all who are
apart
Teaches to give and
forgive
Never binds in fetters
Over comes any fight
by being right
Let hatred be conquered

and gone .

let the fragrance  of love

spread its wings

To bring this essence to

this beautiful world.

## 4. Long for change

When birds chirp aloud
sky appears clear
wind blows mild
so do my heart flows with
wavering emotions
when the leaves fall from
branches
letting the new one's
appear.

when the road leading to

the right path

Comes ahead my wish to

cross the right lane

When the mountains

cover the valley

with the veil of snow

conceal true feelings

But when the water flows

and flows from the brook

So does my heart reveal

My Inner self to you
I long for change.

# 5. LOVE

When in love
We laugh and cry

We are ready to say hello

Sad to say goodbye

We hold hands to prove

How much we care

They are our dear

We learn to forgive and

forget

Proud to feel them

around

We wipe their tears

If they have fear

We tell them we are here

and you may be there

we shall overcome this

distance

Love us till the end.

# 6. Woman

Woman does a lot

Over burdens herself

Angel of the house

Nature made her

With rare virtues

with all warmth in her

heart

Binds everyone

As a daughter keeps

Good character
When a mother
helps children further.
Above all she is a wife
Who sacrifies her life
In all moments
Be they happy or sad .

# 7. My Tender Feelings

My heart beats

when the scene repeats.

Before my own eyes

Death of thousands.

Is this all wise ?

Innocent people being

killed

by men armed to their

full skill.

who will teach them a
lesson
For what they are doing
in their
so called action
None can preach them
As it is beyond their
reach.
My feelings are still
What have I done until.

# 8. Water

Water -Water all I need

But can turn guile indeed

The flow that came and

wrecked

The life of common

people

Homeless,penniless and

outraged

Facing this acrimonious

truth of nature
They stand and stare
and acquiesce reality
Come my dear friends
with both hands together
Pray for the dead
and help those who are
left ahead
Binding them for bright
sunlight
The Life in the future.

# 9. Earthquake

Precious land turned into
devastation with a quake
Death of all hardly awake
Thunder of one second
brought catastrophe
Anguish of pain sounding
there
Now isn't the hour to
waste in deploring

By poring out their
wounds
But to assist with the
miracle
Of your patience
To heal all with your love
and care .

# 10. Bright Star

How I wanted to catch

the star

once in my dream

The brightest one came

and

I screamed

Wait ! Wait ! Lovely star

be my company for an

hour

Shall show you the world

beyond the sky

Could it be true?

Wondered bright star

taking me somewhere

new

Yes we all are waiting for

you

Come close your eyes

Hold me beside

N0! No! said the star and

took me to the sky.

# 11. Grandma

Clad in white dress

Standing near the pillar

I saw Grandma

Her smile so real

The secret of making

All feel dear

When Sitting next to her

I felt strong connection

As she was talking

I was listening
I cherished now those
moments
Though past
But still clinging
To my heart
God bless her always
As she bestower on all
Her tender love and care.

# 12. Jealousy

Jealousy is the strongest
seed

Not to be developed as
good deed

Always keep the mind
clean

from this dirty scene

Intelligence is the source
to keep away this force

love is the way
to keep it away

# 13. REALITY

My tears came i thought
why again?
I was so happy few
minutes away
My eyes just looking at
the scene
All seem to be sleeping
and looking lean
My heart showing me the

truth
They  are all  dead
Who played this dirty
game?
What passion did they
feel ?
They killed them who
were helpless and weak
Why they had to bear
when the path
They had chosen was so
clear

Tears flowing from my
eyes
Many questions pouring
in my mind on this cruel
fabric called life.

# 14. lane

Path to other lane was
immaculate one
I moved ahead but
something pushed me
back
I was in state of reverie as
one step marched
I saw lights touched me

so Bright they were

My inner voice telling me

not to umbrage for what

i am doing

Was it right or

trepidation phase.

Bewilderment

surrounded Alas! I felt to

forget everything and

Enjoy my foot ride to that

lane.

# 15. Sweet Dream

Alone in the narrow Lane

I was walking

the Greenery that was

surrounded was the best I

found

I turn left and then right

The freshness of flowers

Caught me With their

power
The grass that was so
tender When I sat on
I Felt immense Wonder
Such affection received
that no longer  deceived
Little jerk someone gave
I woke up from pleasant
dream
Could it be ever true
I scream!

# 16. Rain

The sky turning into the
veil of blue cloud
Drops of rain about to
start  aloud
Birds finding their shelter
in the tree
Children running under a
shed to cover their head

Could see a bright face
helping
an elderly lady  to cross
the road.
From my room window.
Could see the view
road turning wet
nature at its best
telling me time to rest.

# 17. Call to environment

I hear a call

Which is for me and all

The call is so strong

You can't prove it wrong

To save innocent
creatures

So they can live life in the
future


To let birds fly high  , to
protect nature


By prohibiting buildings
and huge Structures

To let river flow with

huge mountain near

To let trees grow in

endless row


To let everyone breath

the  fresh air

A Gift from God so rare

Hear the Call

Which is for me and all.

# 18. Caste

Bound with question of

race.


We are caught in a web of

vagaries of caste


What is our real face ?

What are we doing ?

Questions one after

another prevailing

Betray we each-other in
the name of caste. and
have a restricted glance
of this world , so vast and
entangled , still with
narrow lanes and twisted
perception.


what are we doing?

All this is vain

Gathering nothing in
gain.

# 19. Corruption

Gravity of corruption
Everything sounds
arduous
Truth remains concealed
and fraudulous
Rage and vent a call of
the moment
Fight for rights a
benchmark of behavior

this decade
Corruption the true
cancer of this century.

# 20. To- Part

To part from your near
ones
Need to have a big heart
The presence of the
person means a lot
So seeing him not around
pains you alot
Sweet memories remain
there till the end

To fondly remember
again and again
It takes time to adjust
Provided you are
prepared first
So these thoughts get
vague and vague
With every new day
Actually goes deeper and
deeper
To stay.

# 21. Satisfaction

Feeling of satisfaction
must be there
otherwise you will never
be comfortable at all
times
He who understands this
will not find any problem
in different fields

Temptation for things

may remain

But balanced mind will

surely make a person

forget them at all times.